ANTIQUE AMERICAN RECIPES

FROM ELIZA LESLIE'S COOKBOOKS

Eliza Leslie, a woman of amazing energy, was born in 1787 at Philadelphia, Pennsylvania. Her father, a friend of Thomas Jefferson and Ben Franklin, was a mathematician and watchmaker and a member of The American Philosophical Society. Mr. Leslie died suddenly when Eliza was 15. His widow, left to provide for five children, managed a boarding house. Eliza, eager to assist, became useful by completing courses at Mrs. Goodfellow's Philadelphia Cooking School. Her new skills proved greatly helpful.

Within several years Eliza determined to be a writer and, in 1828, a Boston publisher issued her first cookbook, *Seventy-Five Receipts for Pastry, Cakes and Sweetmeats*. Rewarded with immediate success she began writing steadily, producing a variety of works including juvenile stories, handbooks on housekeeping and manners, a novel — and eight more cookbooks. She won national popularity and further broadened her career by serving a number of years as associate editor of the famous *Godey's Ladies Book* magazine and editor of *The Gift*, an annual.

Miss Leslie's *Directions for Cookery*, 1837, was the best seller of the 19th century among American cookbooks, with 38 editions.

James Beard said of Miss Leslie, "She was the best cook of her time." And John and Karen Hess in their *The Taste of America* said, "In our view Eliza Leslie's *Directions for Cookery* ranks with Mrs Randolph's *Virginia Housewife* as one of the two best all-American cookbooks ever written."

Eliza Leslie

ANTIQUE AMERICAN RECIPES

FROM ELIZA LESLIE'S COOKBOOKS

Chosen and edited by Hope Peek

CONSTANTIA BOOKS

PRINTED IN THE UNITED STATES OF AMERICA

Published by
Constantia Books
40 Carwall Avenue
Mount Vernon NY 10552
Tel 914 699 5517

CONTENTS

INTRODUCTION

Cooking enthusiasts are presently finding new tastebud kicks in old recipes. One source of treasure is the first half of the 19th century, when the nation was a youngster and a truly American cuisine had its start.

Our ancestors of the period often found cooking a kind of high adventure, since their skills were tested by many unfamiliar foods. Indeed they took all the challenges in stride and handed down a bundle of gastronomic delights. A lot of favorite dishes made their entrance then as a result of neighborly chit-chat with friendly Indians. They introduced the pioneer-settlers to corn, pumpkin, blueberries, cranberries, wild rice, maple syrup, wild duck, turkey, crabs, clams, oysters and catfish.

Other good ideas came from the talents of housewife-cooks among the mix of new citizens from the British Isles, Europe, the Indies and elsewhere. The Dutch, for example, came up with cabbage slaw and scrumptious cookies. Britons concocted irresistible meat and game pies, crumpets, puddings and catchups. French creations featured meat and seafood delicacies, mustards, drinks and ice creams. The Germans invented hearty beef and veal dishes, puddings and cakes. And a distinctive Creole flavor scored conquests with spicy gumbo, molasses and yams.

Our recipe lineup is a sampling of old taste successes that will hopefully generate more revivals and appreciations. Our authority is Eliza Leslie, foremost cookbook writer of the era and a celebrated cook. She was rightly proud of American cooking and her recipes adapt smoothly to the 1980s kitchen.

SOUPS

CATFISH SOUP

Serves 4

1½ pounds catfish fillets	2 tablespoons butter
½ cup diced ham	2 tablespoons flour
½ cup chopped parsley	
3 stalks celery, sliced	2 cups light cream
1 heaping tablespoon fresh marjoram	2 egg yolks
Pepper	Croutons

Cut fish into bite-sized pieces and set aside. In a large pan combine ham, parsley, celery, marjoram, generous grating of pepper and 4 cups water. Bring to boil, cover, and simmer 30 minutes. Add fish. In another pan melt butter, stir in flour, then the cream, and bring to boil—stirring constantly. Pour mix into soup and simmer 15 minutes. Stir some soup liquid into egg yolks and add them to soup. Stir briefly to thicken soup. Serve piping hot, sprinkled with croutons.

GUMBO

Serves 4

*Gumbo is an African word for okra. The word
and the plant came to us via the slave ships.*

3 pounds okra, finely
  chopped

3 pounds ripe tomatoes,
  peeled and chopped

1 onion, minced

2 tablespoons butter

Pepper and salt

4 slices toast, crusts
  removed, cut into
  12 fingers

Combine all ingredients except toast. Simmer, covered, one
hour. To serve, strain into a tureen. Serve toast at table.

OCHRA SOUP

Serves 4

1 pound lean stewing
  beef, diced

½ cup diced boiled ham

¼ cup butter

6 tomatoes, peeled and
  chopped

1 pound okras, sliced
  thin

Salt

Cayenne pepper

1 ten-ounce package
  frozen lima beans

Croutons

Put beef, ham, butter, tomatoes, okras, salt and cayenne into a
pot. Add enough boiling water to cover. Stew, covered, 1 hour
over low heat. Add 3 pints water, bring to boil, then skim off
scum. Cover and simmer 3 hours. Cook lima beans in separate
pan. Strain the soup, add lima beans and sprinkle with croutons.

BEAN SOUP
Serves 4

2 cups white beans
1 pound beef bones
¼ pound lean beef (1-inch pieces)
¼ pound Canadian bacon (1-inch pieces)

Pepper and salt

4 stalks celery, chopped

Croutons

Soak beans overnight. Drain. Combine bones, beef, bacon and 6 cups water in large pot. Season to taste. Bring to boil, then skim off foam. Add beans and celery, cover, and simmer 3 hours. Drain, set liquid aside and discard meat and bones. Puree the beans. Return ingredients to liquid and reheat. Serve from tureen, sprinkling each serving with croutons.

CLAM SOUP

Serves 4

2 pounds veal bones

1 yam, peeled and chopped

1 bouquet garni (parsley, thyme, bay leaf)

1 teaspoon peppercorns

¼ teaspoon each, nutmeg & mace

2 tablespoons butter rubbed into 2 tablespoons flour

1 dozen clams

Croutons

Combine bones, yam, bouquet garni, peppercorns and spices in 4 cups water. Bring to boil, skim off foam, reduce heat, cover, simmer 3 hours. Strain, return liquid to pot and stir in butter-flour mix, a piece at a time. Scrub clams, then open and add their juice. Chop clams, add them to soup and cook 5 minutes. Sprinkle with croutons when serving.

FISH

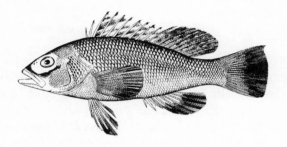

FRIED SEA BASS
Serves 4

1 two-pound sea bass	1 cup chopped parsley
Salt	2 hardboiled eggs, sliced
Cayenne pepper	2 tablespoons butter
½ cup clarified butter	1 tablespoon flour
2 onions, sliced	¼ cup wine vinegar

Cut off head and tail, make 3 slashes on sides of fish, then rub with seasoning. Heat clarified butter and cook fish 5 minutes on each side. Cover a side of fish with onions and parsley and cook another 5 minutes. Repeat for other side. Move fish to heated platter and surround with sliced eggs. Discard butter from pan, replace with fresh butter, stir in flour and vinegar. Heat until brown and pour over fish.

CREAM TROUT
Serves 4

4 trout	1 cup heavy cream
½ teaspoon each mace and nutmeg	1 teaspoon arrowroot
Cayenne pepper	1 tablespoon milk
2 teaspoons grated lemon peel	4 tablespoons lemon juice

Remove heads and tails and poach fish 5 minutes in simmering salted water. Drain. Combine mace, nutmeg and cayenne and rub over fish. Lay fish in a pan, sprinkle with lemon peel, then add cream. Bring to simmer, cover, and cook 10 minutes. Remove fish to heated platter. Mix arrowroot and milk into smooth paste and add to pan liquid, on medium heat. Add lemon juice and stir until sauce thickens. Pour sauce over fish.

BAKED SHAD
Serves 4

1½ pounds shad fillets	⅛ teaspoon mace
2 egg yolks, beaten	Pepper and salt
1 cup fresh breadcrumbs	½ cup port wine
½ cup ground ham	1 tablespoon flour, rubbed with 1 tablespoon butter
½ teaspoon dried marjoram, crushed	Lemon slices

Lay fish in pan and brush with egg yolk. Mix remaining egg yolk with breadcrumbs, ham, marjoram, mace, pepper and salt and spread on fillets. Pour in wine plus ¼ cup water. Bake 15 minutes in 425-degree oven. Remove fish to warm platter. Stir flour-butter mixture, bit by bit, into liquid in pan. Simmer 5 minutes, then pour over fish. Garnish with lemon slices to serve.

6

TO BOIL SALT CODFISH
Serves 4

1 pound boneless salt cod

½ cup molasses

4 hard-boiled eggs

Egg sauce (see below)

Mashed potatoes

Boiled parsnips

Mustard

Cayenne pepper

Soak cod in cold water 48 hours, changing water every 12 hours. Place fish in large saucepan, stir molasses into enough water to cover and add to pan. Bring to boil, lower heat and simmer 20 minutes. Drain fish, cut into pieces and move to warm platter. Surround with sliced eggs. Serve egg sauce at table, accompanied by potatoes, parsnips, mustard and cayenne.

EGG SAUCE

4 tablespoons butter cut in small pieces

1 heaping teaspoon flour

8 tablespoons milk

2 hardboiled eggs

Pepper and salt

In a saucepan rub butter and flour together and combine with 2 tablespoons milk. Place on high heat and stir in remaining milk. Bring to boil, then lower heat and simmer 5 minutes. Chop eggs and stir into sauce. Season to taste.

SCOLLOPED OYSTERS

Serves 4

4 scallop shells	Nutmeg
1 cup fresh breadcrumbs	Cayenne pepper
24 oysters and their juice	3 tablespoons melted butter

Butter 4 scallop shells and sprinkle with breadcrumbs (2 table-spoons). Place 6 oysters in each shell, sprinkle with nutmeg and cayenne and pour in 2 teaspoons of oyster juice. Combine remaining breadcrumbs with butter and spread over oysters. Brown oysters under broiler.

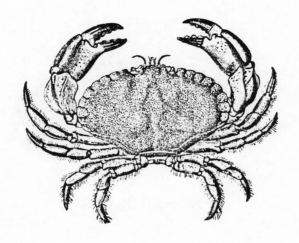

COLD CRABS

Serves 4

1 pound lump crabmeat	1 teaspoon Dijon-style mustard
1 hardboiled egg	Cayenne pepper
2 tablespoons olive oil	Salt
	3 tablespoons vinegar

Place crabmeat on platter. Separate egg yolk from white. Chop white and set aside. Mash egg yolk into oil and add mustard, cayenne and salt. Now add vinegar and whisk until dressing becomes creamy smooth. Pour sauce over crab and sprinkle with chopped egg white. Chill before serving.

9

SOFT CRABS
Serves 4

½ cup parsley sprigs

12 cleaned soft-shell crabs

Seasoned flour

Lard for frying

1 cup cream

¼ cup chopped parsley

Pepper and salt

Wash and dry parsley sprigs and set aside. Dry crabs and dredge in flour. Fry in hot lard until golden brown, then drain on paper towels and keep warm. Re-heat lard and toss in parsley sprigs, turning until crisp. Place crisp parsley with crabs. Now add cream, chopped parsley, pepper and salt to the pan and cook 2 minutes. Stir to mix ingredients well. Serve crabs, covered with crisp parsley, on a platter. Serve sauce at table in a boat.

MEAT

BEEF BOUILLI
Serves 4

3 pounds boneless
bottom round

Salt

1 cup chicken stock

4 carrots, sliced

4 stalks celery, sliced

4 turnips, sliced

1 bouquet garni
(parsley, thyme, bay leaf)

1 tablespoon peppercorns,
wrapped & tied in
cheesecloth

12 pearl onions

1 heaping tablespoon
capers

Catchup (pages 31 & 32)
or Worcestershire sauce

Mustard (page 33)

Place small rack at bottom of large pot. Rub meat generously
with salt and place on rack. Pour in stock and enough water to
cover. Bring to boil over high heat. Skim off foam, lower heat
and add carrots, celery, turnips, bouquet garni and peppercorns.
Cover and simmer 3 hours. Add onions and capers, then simmer
½ hour. Remove bouquet garni and peppercorns. To serve,
arrange sliced beef, surrounded by vegetables, on warm platter.
Spoon some cooking liquid over meat. Serve catchup (or
Worcestershire sauce) and mustard at table.

BEEF CAKES

Serves 4

(A breakfast favorite)

1½ cups diced, cooked roast beef

½ cup diced ham

2 tablespoons breadcrumbs

1 tablespoon chopped onion

1 tablespoon chopped parsley

1 teaspoon juice from pickled onions

3 tablespoons melted butter

Pepper and salt

2 cups cold mashed potatoes

Combine roast beef, ham, breadcrumbs, onion, parsley, pickle juice, 2 tablespoons butter, and seasoning. Put in processor until finely chopped (8 to 10 seconds). Shape mixture into 8 flat cakes, then spread mashed potatoes thinly on top and bottom. Brush tops with remaining butter. Preheat broiler and place the cakes, arranged on buttered baking sheet, on middle oven shelf. Broil until tops are browned (about 5 minutes).

PORK PIE
Serves 4

Flaky pastry

1 pound boneless lean
   pork loin, sliced

Nutmeg

Pepper and salt

3 McIntosh or similar
   apples, peeled, cored
   and chopped

3 teaspoons sugar

¾ cup white wine

Decorations and glaze
(page 65)

Line a 1-quart baking dish with pastry. Make a layer of pork at bottom, sprinkled over with nutmeg, seasoning, apples and a teaspoon of sugar. Add two similar layers and pour in the wine. Make a pastry top, pinch edges to seal and punch a hole in center. Decorate and glaze. Bake in 375-degree oven 1½ hours.

FINE SAUSAGES
Serves 4

⅔ pound lean pork,
   diced

⅓ pound pork fat,
   diced

1 teaspoon salt

½ teaspoon pepper

½ teaspoon sage

¼ teaspoon each cloves,
   mace and nutmeg

⅛ teaspoon crushed
   rosemary

2 egg yolks

Blend all ingredients, except egg yolks, in food processor until semi-smooth. Spoon into wide-mouthed container, press down, cover, and refrigerate 24 hours. To cook, mix in egg yolks, shape into 8 patties and dredge in flour. Fry in butter until brown.

A BEEF-STEAK PIE
Serves 4

Flaky pastry

1 pound sirloin, fat removed, sliced into thin, small pieces (seasoned with salt and pepper)

2 medium potatoes, peeled and thinly sliced

2 tablespoons butter, rubbed into 2 tablespoons flour

1½ cups sliced mushrooms

Decorations and glaze (page 65)

Line a buttered quart-size baking dish with pastry. Make nine layers for the pie, as follows: Layer of meat, topped by layer of potatoes (dotted with butter-flour mix), topped by layer of mushrooms. Repeat this two more times. Pour ½ cup of water over layers. Add pastry cover, notch edges, punch a hole at top center, decorate and glaze. Bake 1½ hours in a 375-degree oven.

VEAL CUTLETS
Serves 4

8 veal scallops

Pepper and salt

¼ teaspoon saffron threads

2 cups stale breadcrumbs

1 tablespoon minced fresh marjoram

1 tablespoon grated lemon peel

½ teaspoon mace

2 eggs, beaten

Butter for frying

1 tablespoon butter

1 tablespoon flour

1 cup beef broth

Parsley sprigs for garnish

Season the cutlets. Crumble saffron and combine with breadcrumbs, marjoram, lemon peel and mace. Dip cutlets into egg, then into crumb mixture and let stand 10 minutes. Fry meat on both sides until brown and transfer to warm platter. Discard butter in pan, heat some fresh butter, then add flour and beef broth and cook 5 minutes — to make gravy. To serve, pour gravy around cutlets and garnish with parsley.

CUTLETS A LA MAINTENON
Serves 4

8 rib lamb chops, "Frenched" (rib bone free of meat and fat, chopped short)

8 squares cooking foil

4 tablespoons melted butter

½ cup fresh breadcrumbs

2 hardboiled egg yolks, crumbled

2 tablespoons minced onion

2 tablespoons minced parsley

1 teaspoon each, minced fresh thyme and marjoram

¼ teaspoon nutmeg

Pepper and salt

Gravy (see below)

Flatten chops with cleaver, then brush the chops and foil with butter. Mix remaining ingredients, except gravy, and coat chops with the mixture. Place each chop diagonally on a foil square, fold over to make container and seal edges. Broil chops 7 minutes on each side. Open and remove foil. Serve gravy at table.

GRAVY

1 tablespoon butter

1 tablespoon browned flour

¾ cup beef broth

¼ cup red wine

Melt butter, stir in flour, broth and wine. Bring to boil, while whisking, then lower heat and simmer 15 minutes.

15

TO STEW A ROUND OF BEEF
Serves 4

3 pounds boneless bottom-
  round of beef

Salt

Cider vinegar

6 tablespoons butter

2 cups port wine

2 onions, sliced

3 cloves

1 tablespoon black
  peppercorns

3 tablespoons flour

Rub beef with salt and place in a bowl. Mix equal parts of vinegar and water and pour over meat. Let stand 24 hours, turning meat several times. Remove meat and dry thoroughly. Melt 3 tablespoons butter in a large pot, then brown the meat on all sides. Pour off butter and add 1½ cups port wine, onions, cloves, peppercorns and 2 cups water. Cover and simmer 3 hours. Remove meat and onions to a warm platter. De-grease and strain cooking liquid. In another pan melt remaining butter, stir in flour, remainder of wine and 2½ cups cooking liquid. Stir this until smooth. Slice the meat, surround with onions and spoon some sauce over it. Serve remainder of sauce at table.

TO STEW A BREAST OF VEAL
Serves 4

1 large onion, sliced	2½ pounds veal breast (2-inch pieces)
2 cups parsley sprigs	2 tomatoes, peeled, seeded, chopped
1½ cups chopped ham	1½ cups green peas
12 peppercorns	1 tablespoon flour, rubbed into a tablespoon butter

In a large pot layer onion, parsley, ham, pepper, veal and tomatoes — and pour in ½ cup water. Cover and cook over very low heat 2½ hours. Add peas during last 15 minutes of cooking. Place veal on heated platter and border it with peas. Stir flour-butter mix, a piece at a time, into liquid in pan and simmer 5 minutes. To serve, spoon sauce over veal.

PORK CHEESE
Serves 8

4 pigs feet

2 pounds lean pork, diced

4 fresh sage leaves, chopped

4 tablespoons chopped fresh marjoram

¼ teaspoon powdered cloves

Pepper and salt

Mustard (page 33)

Malt vinegar

Place pigs feet and pork in a pot with water to cover. Bring slowly to boil over medium heat. Skim off foam, cover, lower heat and simmer 4 hours. Discard pigs feet. Remove pork and set aside. Reserve liquid. Wipe out pot, then return liquid to it and add sage, marjoram, cloves and seasoning. Reduce liquid by half over high heat, then add pork. Now quickly transfer contents to an oiled loaf-pan. Let this cool. Meanwhile, cut a cardboard shape as a lid for the loaf-pan and wrap it in foil. Press the lid tightly against the meat and put a weight on top. Refrigerate overnight. To serve, unmold the jellied meat to a platter and slice it. Accompany with mustard and vinegar.

18

POULTRY & GAME

TO ROAST GAME BIRDS
Serves 4

4 game hens	4 slices bacon
Pepper and salt	1 tablespoon browned flour
4 oranges	1 cup red wine

Sprinkle seasoning inside each bird and stuff with one-half a peeled, seeded, sliced orange. Truss birds. Cut bacon slices in half and place on breasts, secured with toothpicks. Put birds on rack of roasting pan. Take juice of remaining oranges, add ½ cup water and pour over birds. Roast 1¼ hours in 350-degree oven, basting frequently with pan liquid. Remove birds to platter, untruss and remove toothpicks. Stir flour and wine into pan liquid and simmer several minutes. To serve, spoon sauce over birds and provide additional sauce at table.

FRICASSEED CHICKEN

Serves 4

1 four-pound chicken	Forcemeat balls
½ teaspoon marjoram	(see below)
¼ teaspoon each, nutmeg and mace	1 tablespoon butter rubbed into 1 tablespoon flour
Pepper and salt	
2 cups half-and-half cream	Fried parsley (see below)

Skin chicken, remove fat and cut into serving portions. Soak in cold salted water overnight. Drain. Put into pot with seasoning and cream, cover, and simmer over low heat 1½ hours. Add forcemeat balls and simmer 15 minutes. Remove chicken and meatballs to heated platter. Stir butter-flour mix into sauce in pan, a piece at a time. To serve, pour sauce over chicken, garnish with fried parsley and offer additional sauce at table.

FORCEMEAT BALLS

½ pound ground veal	⅛ teaspoon each nutmeg and mace
1 egg, beaten slightly	
¼ teaspoon marjoram	Pepper and salt

Mix ingredients, then roll into 8 or more small ball shapes.

FRIED PARSLEY

Parsley sprigs   Lard

Soak parsley 1 hour in icewater. Dry thoroughly. Heat 1-inch deep portion of lard in frying pan, add a few sprigs of parsley, cook several seconds and remove with slotted spoon. Repeat for quantity wanted. Drain on paper towels.

A PILAU
Serves 4

*Pilau, pronounced payloss, originated
in the old rice plantations around
Charleston, South Carolina*

1 three-pound chicken	½ teaspoon mace
2 slices bacon	White pepper
2 onions, sliced	
1½ cups long-grain rice	Salt

Truss the chicken and place it breast-side-down in a pot. Pour in 4 cups boiling water, cover, and simmer ½ hour. Remove from pot and reserve cooking liquid. Chop 1 slice of bacon and melt over low heat. Add onions and cook until soft. Cover chicken breast with remaining bacon slice, secure with toothpicks, and place in pot. Pour rice around chicken and add onions, mace, pepper and salt. Measure 3½ cups cooking liquid, heat to boiling and pour over rice. Cover and simmer ½ hour. To serve, heap rice on a platter, untruss chicken, remove bacon, cut chicken into pieces and arrange over rice.

TO HASH A DUCK
Serves 4

1 five-pound duck,
   cut in pieces

Allspice

Pepper

8 slices ham

1 cup red wine

3 cups green peas

Butter

Skin and de-fat duck and discard the back. Season duck pieces with allspice and pepper. Lay half the ham at bottom of a pot and cover with duck. Add layer of ham on top. Pour in wine and ¼ cup water. Bring to simmer, cover, and cook 1 hour. Cook peas, seasoned with butter and pepper. Serve the layered dish on a platter, surrounded by peas.

COUNTRY CAPTAIN
Serves 4

4 cups chicken broth

4 chicken breasts

2 onions, sliced

2 tablespoons curry
   powder

½ cup clarified butter

4 tablespoons grated
   fresh coconut

Boiled long-grain rice

Heat broth to a simmer, add chicken, cover, and poach 15 minutes. Remove chicken and set aside. Reheat broth to a simmer and poach onions 5 minutes. Drain and set onions aside. Rub chicken with curry powder and fry in hot butter until brown, then transfer to a heated platter. Combine onions and cocnut and fry until coconut is light brown. Surround chicken with onion-coconut mix. Serve boiled rice separately.

CHICKEN SALAD

Serves 4

A fine, appetising supper dish. Teams well with shellfish: soft crabs, lobster, oysters and shrimp.

1 boiled or roasted chicken, cold

1 head celery

4 hardboiled eggs

2 teaspoons Dijon-style mustard

½ cup olive oil

2 tablespoons white wine vinegar

Cayenne pepper

Salt

Remove skin and bones from chicken, then cut the meat into bite-size pieces. Cut celery into 1-inch pieces. Mix chicken and celery, cover, and set aside. Separate yolks and whites of eggs. Slice egg whites into rings and reserve. Blend egg yolks with 1 tablespoon water until smooth. Add to this mustard, olive oil, vinegar, cayenne and salt and beat until creamy. Spoon sauce over chicken-celery mix, then toss well. When serving, decorate top with egg rings.

VEGETABLES

STEWED EGGPLANT

Serves 4

*"Generally a breakfast dish
but sometimes eaten at dinner."*

1 large eggplant	½ teaspoon marjoram
½ cup fresh breadcrumbs	⅛ teaspoon powdered cloves
3 tablespoons melted butter	Pepper and salt

Peel eggplant and cut into cubes. Cover with boiling water and cook until soft. Drain and mash. Stir in 2 tablespoons bread-crumbs, 2 tablespoons butter, marjoram, cloves and seasoning — and place in baking dish. Toss remaining breadcrumbs with butter and sprinkle on top. Bake in 475-degree oven 15 minutes.

STEWED TOMATAS
Serves 4

4 pounds tomatoes, peeled, seeded and chopped

2 tablespoons minced onions

¼ teaspoon mace

Cayenne pepper

Salt

Combine all ingredients in a saucepan and cook over low heat until thick. Serve warm.

PORK AND BEANS

This homely dish is universally much liked. It is customarily brought to table in the dish in which it was baked.

2 cups white beans

½ pound salt pork

Pepper

Soak beans overnight in enough water to cover. Drain. Place in pot and add fresh water to cover. Wash and dry salt pork and arrange in strips over beans. Season generously with pepper. Bring to boil, skim off foam, then simmer on low heat 2 hours, adding water as needed. Remove from heat, transfer beans to baking dish (with pork on top). Bake in 225-degree oven 4 hours. Serve very hot.

MOCK OYSTERS OF CORN
Serves 4

*"An excellent relish at breakfast, or
a side-dish at dinner. Has a singular
resemblance to fried oysters."*

1 ten-ounce package frozen corn	2 egg yolks
	Lard
4 tablespoons flour	Butter

Thaw the corn, then place in food processor with flour and egg yolks and process until smooth. Using a tablespoon drop portions of corn into a 50-50 mixture of hot lard and butter. Cook to golden brown, drain on paper towels. Makes 12 "oysters."

ONION CUSTARD
Serves 4

5 medium onions, sliced	2 eggs
	1 cup milk
2 tablespoons butter	½ teaspoon nutmeg

Cook onions slowly in butter until they reach rich brown color. Drain and puree. Beat eggs, stir into milk, then add onions and nutmeg. Pour mix into 1-quart baking dish and bake 40 minutes in 375-degree oven.

WARM SLAW
Serves 4

1 head red cabbage	1 clove garlic, minced
¼ cup butter	Cayenne pepper
2 tablespoons vinegar	Salt

Shred cabbage, then place in ovenproof bowl, cover and cook in warm oven ½ hour. Combine butter, vinegar, garlic and seasoning with ¾ cup water. Boil 5 minutes and pour over cabbage. Mix well before serving.

SAUCES

PEACH SAUCE

Yields about 2 cups

1 seven-ounce package
   dried peaches

½ cup brown sugar

Soak peaches overnight in enough water to cover. Drain and transfer to pan containing ¼ cup water. Cover and simmer over very low heat until fruit is liquefied, then stir in sugar. Let stand until cool. *(Excellent accompaniment to roast meat, game or poultry.)*

COLD SWEET SAUCE

½ cup softened butter
½ cup powdered sugar

¼ teaspoon cinnamon
4 drops lemon extract

Cream the butter and gradually sift in sugar. Beat mix until fluffy and add cinnamon and lemon extract. Continue to beat until creamy smooth, then chill. Send to table in a deep plate accompanied by teaspoon. *(A very nice sauce for Indian pudding, other puddings and pancakes.)*

SALAD DRESSING

2 hardboiled eggs	1 teaspoon sugar
2 tablespoons olive oil	Salt
1 teaspoon Dijon-style mustard	2 tablespoons vinegar

Separate egg yolks and whites. Slice whites into rings and set aside. Mash yolks with 1 tablespoon water, then add, while whisking, olive oil, mustard, sugar, salt and vinegar. Beat until smooth. To serve, pour over salad, toss, then decorate top of greens with egg-white rings.

CRANBERRY SAUCE

4 cups cranberries	2 cups brown sugar

Wash cranberries and combine with sugar and ¼ cup water in a pot. Stew over high heat, stirring constantly, until berries burst and sauce is marmelade-like. Let stand until cool. *(To prepare as a jelly, strain and mash the berries, by sieving, into an oiled mold. Refrigerate until contents are firm, then unmold onto a plate.)*

CATCHUPS & MUSTARDS

SEA CATCHUP

*This catchup keeps well, for example, at sea,
and may be carried across the world. A spoonful
mixed with melted butter makes a superb fish sauce.
It is also a fine flavoring for gravy.*

1 quart stale beer	¼ pound shallots, chopped
1 pound mushrooms, minced	8 peppercorns
	4 whole cloves
¼ pound anchovies, washed and chopped	2 blades mace
	1 large piece ginger-root

Mix all ingredients in a large saucepan and boil, covered, until
quantity is reduced by half. Strain, let stand to cool, then bottle
for storage.

PUDDING CATCHUP

1 cup noyau (page 63)

2 cups sherry

Peel of 4 lemons

1 tablespoon mace

½ cup sugar

Combine noyau, sherry, lemon peel and mace and let stand 2 weeks. Strain. Boil sugar in ½ cup water (until dissolved), then add to noyau-sherry mix. When using the sauce for a pudding, melt 2 tablespoons butter, stir in a teaspoon of flour and a cup of catchup. Bring to boil, while stirring, then remove from heat. Serve warm and pour over puddings or ice cream.

LEMON CATCHUP

5 lemons

2 tablespoons mustard seeds

1 tablespoon black peppercorns

½ tablespoon whole mace

½ tablespoon whole cloves

1 whole nutmeg

1 tablespoon salt

2 tablespoons sliced horseradish root

2 cups white wine vinegar

Slice lemons and remove seeds. Wrap spices in towel and hammer surface to crush them. Combine lemons, spice mix, salt, horseradish and vinegar in saucepan and boil 20 minutes. Pour into quart-jar, cover and let stand to cool. Refrigerate 3 weeks, during which time shake jar a few seconds each day. Strain, discard solids and bottle the liquid. Makes an unusually good sauce for chicken, fish and vegetables.

FRENCH MUSTARD

½ cup dry mustard

1 heaping tablespoon minced fresh tarragon (or 1 teaspoon dried)

2 cloves garlic, mashed

½ teaspoon salt

¼ cup tarragon vinegar

Blend together mustard, tarragon, garlic and salt. Add vinegar, then whisk until mixture is smooth and creamy. Transfer to a jar with tight stopper. Refrigerate two days.

KEEPING MUSTARD

1 teaspoon salt

½ cup vinegar

2 teaspoons grated fresh horseradish root

6 tablespoons dry mustard

Dissolve salt in boiling vinegar, then stir in horseradish. Remove from heat, pour into a bowl, cover with foil and let stand 24 hours. Strain, add mustard and beat into velvety smoothness. Store in wide-mouth jar with tight top.

PICKLES & PRESERVES

PICKLED EGGS

1 dozen eggs

3 cups white wine vinegar

1 whole nutmeg, cracked

1 tablespoon peppercorns

1 teaspoon each, whole cloves and mace

¼ teaspoon almond extract

1 small piece fresh ginger-root

Boil eggs, rinse under cold water and shell. Put them into large jar (glass or stoneware) with non-metal lid. Combine vinegar and spices in a saucepan, bring to boil, then pour over eggs. Cover and let stand 3 days. Return vinegar and spices to saucepan and bring to boil. Now, again, pour this over eggs, replace jar lid and let stand 2 weeks in a cool place.

TOMATA HONEY
Yields 5 jars

4 pounds ripe tomatoes	Lemon juice (liquid from 1 lemon per cup of tomato juice)
Lemon peel, grated (1 lemon per pound of tomatoes)	
Sugar (1 cup per cup of tomato juice)	Almond extract (2 drops per cup of tomato juice)

Chop tomatoes coarsely, add lemon peel, cover and simmer until tomatoes are pulped. Strain and squeeze through sieve lined with 2 layers of damp cheesecloth. Measure juice to determine balance of sugar, etc. Combine tomato juice, sugar, lemon juice and almond extract in large pot, bring to boil and boil hard 50 minutes — while stirring frequently. Pour the honey into clean, hot 8-ounce domed jars, allowing ⅛-inch "headroom." Cover with screw caps, let stand to cool, then store.

(This jelly, which has a honey taste, enhances pork and lamb dishes.)

PUMPKIN CHIPS

1 pumpkin	Lemon juice (½ cup per pound of pumpkin)
Sugar (2 cups per pound of pumpkin)	1 tablespoon lemon peel, slivered

Peel the pumpkin, remove strings and seeds and slice into very thin chips. Weigh chips, in connection with balancing ingredients, then spread in a flat pan. Sprinkle with sugar and lemon juice, stir, cover, and let stand overnight. Transfer to large pan, add lemon peel, bring to boil, skim off foam and cook 45 minutes. Remove from heat and let stand to cool. Pack chips to store in wide-mouth pint jars, covered with syrup, and sealed.

PEACH JELLY
Yields 4 jars

5 pounds freestone
 peaches

Sugar (1 cup per cup of
 peach juice)

Almond extract (2 drops
 per cup of peach juice)

6 ounces fruit pectin

Pit and chop peaches, add ½ cup water, cover, stir and simmer 5 minutes. Put fruit in damp jelly bag and hang to drip until juice is extracted. Measure quantity of juice by cups and pour into large saucepan. Add required sugar and almond extract. Bring to boil over high heat, stirring constantly, and add pectin. Continue cooking at rolling boil level 10 minutes — while stirring. Remove from heat, skim off foam, ladle into hot, sterile 8-ounce domed jelly jars. Allow ⅛-inch "headroom" at top. Screw on jar lids and let stand to cool.

APPLE BUTTER
Yields 1 quart

A tasty compound of apples and cider boiled together to make a preserve with the consistency of soft butter. Can be made only from fresh cider. A very good addition to tea or luncheon.

4 cups new cider

4 pounds eating
 apples

1 teaspoon cinnamon

¼ teaspoon each
 cloves and nutmeg

Boil cider until quantity is reduced by half. Peel, core and quarter apples, then simmer several hours, in cider, on low heat. Stir constantly to avoid scorching. When apples are mushy and darkish brown the cooking is nearly completed. Now stir in the spices and cook another 30 minutes. Let stand to cool, then spoon the "butter" into sterilized jars and put lids on tightly. Apple butter will keep as long as a year.

BREAKFAST &
TEA CAKES

FLANNEL CAKES
Yields 8 cakes

1 package active dry
yeast

2 cups lukewarm milk

1 tablespoon melted
butter

2 cups flour

1 teaspoon salt

2 large or 3 small
eggs

Sprinkle the yeast into ½ cup warm water and stir. Let stand 15 minutes, then whisk to a creamy froth. Stir in milk and butter. Sift flour and combine with salt, then stir into the milk-yeast mixture. Cover batter and allow to rise 2 to 3 hours (until batter is light and bubbly). Beat eggs until frothy and stir into batter. Heat griddle, grease lightly and pour batter for one cake (6 inches across). When bubbles appear on surface, turn over and cook other side. Stack cakes in warm oven until batch is completed. (Batter, minus the eggs, may be prepared day before and kept overnight before use. In the morning, remove from refrigerator, add eggs, stir well and let stand 1 hour.)

RICE CAKES
Yields 12

1½ cups flour	¼ teaspoon salt
1½ cups cold cooked long-grain rice	2 eggs
½ cup melted butter	2 cups milk

Sift flour over rice and combine with butter and salt. Beat the eggs and stir into milk, then add to rice mix and beat until smooth. Pour batter into buttered muffin tins and bake 25 minutes in a 425-degree oven. Serve hot with butter and honey (or molasses).

INDIAN CRUMPETS
Yields 16 or more cakes

1 package active dry yeast	½ teaspoon salt
2 cups cornmeal	1¾ cups milk
1 cup flour	1 egg, plus 1 egg yolk

Sprinkle the yeast into ¼ cup warm water and stir. Let stand 15 minutes, then whisk to a creamy froth. Combine by sifting the cornmeal, flour and salt and warm 5 minutes in a slow oven. Warm the milk, beat the eggs and combine these. Now mix together the cornmeal, yeast and milk — beating constantly. Cover batter and allow it to rise until light and bubbly, then stir. Heat the griddle, grease it lightly and pour batter for 4 small cakes. When cake surface bubbles turn over and cook other side. Stack cakes in warm oven until batch is completed. Serve warm with butter and molasses or honey.

40

INDIAN FLAPPERS
Yields 20 or more cakes

1 cup cornmeal	2 eggs
2 tablespoons flour	2 cups milk
¾ teaspoon salt	Melted butter

Sift cornmeal, flour and salt together. Beat eggs, stir them into milk and add cornmeal-flour mix. Heat griddle, grease it lightly, then pour batter for 3 or 4 small cakes. When cake surface bubbles turn over and cook on other side. Brush tops with melted butter and stack in warm oven until batch is completed. Stir batter each time cakes are poured. Serve warm with honey, maple syrup or molasses.

TENNESSEE MUFFINS
Yields 12

2 cups cornmeal   Salt

2 eggs, separated

Sift the cornmeal, then put a cup of meal in a bowl. Pour in 2 cups boiling water and let stand until cool. Beat egg yolks well and egg whites until stiff. Add remaining cornmeal to the bowl, salt to taste, and stir in the egg yolks. If batter seems too thick add some water. Fold in egg whites, then spoon the batter into buttered muffin tins and bake 25 minutes in a 425-degree oven.

INDIAN LOAF CAKE
Serves 4

2 cups cornmeal

1½ cups half-and-half cream

½ tablespoon powdered sugar

2 tablespoons butter

Salt

1 teaspoon active dry yeast

2 eggs

Sift cornmeal and set aside. Mix cream, sugar, butter and salt in a saucepan. Heat until tiny bubbles appear around edge of pan, then pour into mixing bowl, add cornmeal and beat thoroughly. Let stand until lukewarm. Sprinkle yeast into ¼ cup warm water, while stirring, let stand 15 minutes, then whisk to a creamy froth. Add yeast and eggs to cornmeal and beat vigorously. Pour batter into well-buttered 6-cup turban mold (or tube pan), cover with a towel and let dough rise until it nearly reaches top of pan (about 1 hour). Now bake 1 hour in 350-degree oven.
(Cornmeal tends to stick to pans during cooking. To avoid this, spray the pan with a non-stick vegetable compound.)

CAKES & COOKIES

HONEY GINGER CAKE

1½ cups softened butter	5 eggs
1¾ cups flour	2 cups honey
2 heaping tablespoons powdered ginger	1 teaspoon baking powder
¼ cup brown sugar	1 tablespoon caraway seeds (optional)

Cream butter until light and fluffy, then sift flour and ginger and stir into butter. Add sugar, well-beaten eggs and honey to mixture (a little egg, then a little honey at a time). Sprinkle baking powder over mix, then beat thoroughly while stirring in caraway seeds. Pour into buttered 9 x 9 x 2-inch baking pan. Cover with foil and bake 30 minutes in 350-degree oven. Now remove foil and bake another 30 minutes.

INDIAN POUND CAKE

1 cup cornmeal	½ teaspoon cinnamon
½ cup flour	2 tablespoons sweet white wine
½ cup softened butter	
½ cup powdered sugar	2 tablespoons brandy
½ teaspoon nutmeg	4 eggs

Sift cornmeal and flour together. Cream the butter and sugar and combine them with spices, wine and brandy. Now beat the eggs and add them, alternately with the cornmeal-flour mix, to the butter-sugar mix. Beat the batter thoroughly, then pour into a buttered loaf-pan and bake 90 minutes in a 300-degree oven.

FRANKLIN CAKE

Yields 12 cakes

Makes a moist, dense cake.
Has outstanding "keeping" quality.

1 cup molasses	½ teaspoon cinnamon
½ cup milk	¼ teaspoon each, cloves and nutmeg
¼ cup melted butter	
6 tablespoons brown sugar	3 eggs
	1½ cups flour
1 teaspoon ginger	Grated peel and juice of 1 orange

Mix molasses, milk and butter in a bowl, then stir in sugar and spices. Add eggs, while beating and alternately sifting flour into mix. Add orange peel and juice. Apportion dough into buttered muffin tins and bake 40 minutes in 350-degree oven. Turn out on cooling racks.

MORAVIAN SUGAR CAKE

1	package active dry yeast	¼	teaspoon salt
¾	cup butter	1	egg, beaten
2	cups warm half-and-half cream	3	tablespoons cinnamon
5½	cups flour	⅔	cup brown sugar
			Granulated sugar

Sprinkle yeast into ½ cup warm water, stir and let stand 15 minutes. Cut up ½ cup butter and blend with the warm cream. Sift 3 cups flour, combine with salt, in a large bowl. Stir in the yeast, then the butter-cream mix. Beat this until smooth, cover, and allow to rise until bulk doubles (2 hours). Stir in egg, sift remaining flour with 1 tablespoon cinnamon and knead into dough. Divide dough into halves and place each half in a buttered square cake tin. Cover and allow to rise as before. Blend brown sugar with remaining butter and cinnamon. Punch about 12 finger-size holes in top of each cake (in even rows) and fill with sugar-butter mix. Now close holes by pinching. Sprinkle tops with granulated sugar and bake 30 minutes in 400-degree oven. Turn out on rack to cool.

COCONUT JUMBLES

1 cup sifted flour

½ cup softened butter

1 egg, plus 1 egg yolk, beaten

1 teaspoon rosewater*

3 cups grated fresh coconut

Powdered sugar

Rub flour into butter, then stir in eggs and rosewater. Add coconut by spoonfuls. Dust hands and pastry board with flour and divide dough into 16 portions. Roll each into narrow roll and form rings by joining ends. Dust each with sugar. Arrange on two buttered baking tins and cook 10 minutes in 450-degree oven.

*Available at specialty food shops.

GROUND-NUT MACCAROONS
Yields 12

1 cup roasted, skinned peanuts

3 egg whites

1 cup powdered sugar (some for sifting)

¼ teaspoon each mace and nutmeg

Grind peanuts and blend with 1 egg white, stirring until smooth. Beat in sugar, spices and nuts, a spoonful at a time. Whip remaining egg whites until semi-dry and fold into mixture. Line baking sheet with unglazed paper. Flour your hands and form small ball shapes with the dough. Place them on baking sheet, 1½ inches apart, and press each into position. Sift sugar over each. Bake 25 minutes in 350-degree oven.

NEW YORK COOKIES

*A contribution of New York's early Dutch settlers.
"Cookie" comes from their "koekje"—little cake.*

¼ cup powdered sugar	½ cup butter
1½ cups flour	1 tablespoon rosewater*
¼ teaspoon baking powder	
¾ teaspoon nutmeg	¾ teaspoon caraway seeds (optional)
¼ teaspoon cinnamon	A wooden cookie print

Dissolve sugar in ¼ cup cold water. Sift flour and combine with baking powder, nutmeg and cinnamon. Cream butter and beat in sugar-water, also flour mixture, rosewater and seeds. Knead dough until light and roll out ½-inch thick. Cut into squares and stamp each with the decorative print. Bake ½ hour on a buttered baking sheet in 375-degree oven.

Available from specialty food shops.

DESSERTS

BIRD'S NEST PUDDING
Serves 4

4 McIntosh or equivalent apples

Lemon juice

8 tablespoons brown sugar

4 lemon slices

3 eggs

1 tablespoon flour

¼ teaspoon almond extract

¼ teaspoon allspice

2 cups milk

Core and peel apples and rub with lemon juice. Place them in 6-cup, round baking dish. Moisten with several tablespoons water, cover, and bake 30 minutes in 350-degree oven. Pour off moisture. Drop tablespoon brown sugar in center each apple, then insert lemon slice in center. Beat eggs and combine with remaining sugar, flour, almond extract and allspice. Scald the milk and pour it, little by little, over egg mix, stirring constantly. Now pour milk-egg mix around apples. Bake additional 30 minutes in 350-degree oven. Cool before serving.

A FARMER'S RICE PUDDING
Serves 4

½ cup long-grain rice	¼ cup brown sugar
2 cups half-and-half cream	1 teaspoon cinnamon

Combine all ingredients in 1-quart baking dish. Bake 2 hours in 300-degree oven. Serve cold.

CINDERELLAS (German Puffs)
Serves 4

4 tablespoons flour	1 cup light cream
½ teaspoon nutmeg	4 eggs
¼ teaspoon cinnamon	Sugar
¼ cup butter	Sauce (see below)

Pre-heat oven to 475-degrees. Sift flour, nutmeg and cinnamon together. Cut butter in small pieces and melt slowly in cream. Beat eggs until foamy, stir eggs and flour, gradually, into cream-butter mix. Beat batter until smooth. Fill 6 buttered custard cups two-thirds full, bake 15 minutes, then turn out on a dish and sprinkle with sugar. Serve hot with sauce (or butter and molasses).

SAUCE

¾ cup heavy cream	2 tablespoons sugar
¼ cup sweet sherry	Nutmeg

Combine all ingredients and heat several minutes.

AN OMELETTE SOUFFLE
Serves 4

*"A very nice and delicate thing when properly managed.
The safest way to avoid failure is to hire a French cook
to come to your kitchen while the first part of dinner
is progressing in the dining room."*

4 eggs, separated

¾ cup powdered sugar

3 tablespoons orange-
flower water

Beat egg yolks until thick, then beat in sugar and orange-flower
water. Beat egg whites until stiff and fold into yolk mix. Bake 40
minutes in 325-degree oven. Serve immediately.

YANKEE APPLE PUDDING
Serves 4

4 McIntosh or
similar apples

½ cup sugar

½ teaspoon baking soda

1 cup sour cream

Flaky pastry

Peel, core and quarter apples. Place one-third in a buttered
1-quart baking dish. Sprinkle ⅓ of sugar over apples. Stir baking
soda into sour cream and pour ⅓ of this over apples. Repeat
process 2 more times. Top with pastry, notch and seal edges and
prick top. Bake in 350-degree oven 1 hour. Serve warm.

PINK CHAMPAGNE JELLY

Serves 4

1 package unflavored gelatin

½ cup bottled still water

½ cup sugar

Red food coloring

1½ cups pink champagne

1 tablespoon lemon juice

Soften gelatin in 2 tablespoons boiling water. Combine sugar and remaining water in saucepan and add food coloring. Boil until sugar is dissolved, add gelatin and stir until it is dissolved. Add champagne and lemon juice, while stirring, then refrigerate until jelly is set. To serve, chop jelly coarsely and spoon into stemmed glass bowls.

BAKED CORNMEAL PUDDING

Serves 4

1 cup cornmeal	¼ cup currants, dredged in flour
1 cup milk	¼ teaspoon each cinnamon and nutmeg
¼ cup butter	Grated peel of ½ orange
½ cup molasses	Cold Sweet Sauce (page 29)
2 eggs	

Sift cornmeal into bowl. Heat milk to boil and pour over meal, stirring well. Cut up butter in saucepan, add molasses and heat until butter is soft. Add to this cornmeal mix, then allow to cool. Beat eggs and stir into cornmeal mix. Next, stir in currants, spices and orange peel. Pour whole pudding into buttered 1-quart baking dish and cook 2 hours in 275-degree oven. Serve warm topped with Cold Sweet Sauce.

RHUBARB CUPS
Serves 6

1 pound rhubarb

1 cup brown sugar

⅓ cup long-grain rice

Cold sweet sauce
(page 29)

Cut rhubarb into 1-inch pieces and cook, covered, in a cup of water until soft. Drain thoroughly. Mash rhubarb, then stir in sugar. Cool. Simmer rice in 2 cups water, until soft and semi-dry, then add to rhubarb. Mix well. Spoon rhubarb into 6 oiled custard cups and refrigerate 4 hours. A half hour before serving unmold onto plates. Top each serving with sauce.

QUINCE FLORENTINE
Serves 6

4 quinces

1 cup sugar

½ cup sweet butter, softened

4 eggs

2 tablespoons rosewater*

½ teaspoon nutmeg

Powdered sugar

Peel, core and chop quinces. Stew in double-boiler with a little water until soft. Mash quinces combined with ½ cup sugar, then cool. Cream the butter and remaining sugar and set aside. Beat eggs until thick and add them and the quince, alternately, to butter-sugar mix. Stir in rosewater and nutmeg. Pour mixture into a buttered 1-quart baking dish and bake 45 minutes in 325-degree oven. Cool. Dust with powdered sugar.

*Available at specialty food shops

YAM PUDDING
Serves 4

½ pound yams
1 cup heavy cream
½ cup sugar
2 tablespoons sherry
2 tablespoons rosewater*

1 teaspoon nutmeg
½ teaspoon cinnamon
3 eggs
Powdered sugar
Pudding catchup sauce (page 32)

Roast yams until soft, then peel and mash. Combine yams with cream, sugar, sherry, rosewater and spices — and mix well. Cool. Beat eggs until foamy and stir into mixture. Place mixture in a buttered 1½-pint baking dish and cook 45 minutes in 375-degree oven. Cool. Sprinkle with powdered sugar and serve with warm Pudding catchup sauce (or Cold sweet sauce, page 29).

*Available at specialty food shops

ICE CREAMS

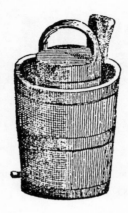

FROZEN CUSTARD
Serves 4

½ a vanilla bean
2 cups milk
2 cups heavy cream

½ cup powdered sugar
1 tablespoon flour
1 egg

Split the vanilla bean, scrape out seeds, then scald them and the pod in ½ cup milk. Discard pod and reserve milk. Do not strain. Mix cream and 1 cup milk and scald. Combine sugar, flour and remaining milk and heat gently until smooth. Now add the cream-milk mix, while stirring, and cook 5 minutes. Beat egg, combine it with 2 tablespoons of hot liquid, while whisking, and add it gently to cream mixture. Now cook 2 minutes while stirring constantly. Remove from heat and stir in vanilla mix. Allow custard to cool, then refrigerate until well chilled. Transfer to ice cream maker and process.

STRAWBERRY ICE CREAM
Serves 4

1 pint ripe strawberries	1 pint heavy
½ cup powdered sugar	cream

Wash and hull strawberries and place in a deep dish. Add ¼ cup sugar, stir, cover, and let stand 2 hours. Stir several times while standing. Mash berries through a sieve, then stir in remaining sugar and cream. Chill, then transfer to ice cream maker and process according to manufacturer's instructions.

ALMOND ICE CREAM
Serves 4

¾ cup almond paste	¼ cup powdered sugar
2½ cups heavy cream	2 teaspoons rosewater*

Place almond paste and ¾ cup cream in a saucepan, mix thoroughly and heat to boiling, while stirring. Stir in sugar, then allow to cool. Now, stir in rosewater, beat remaining cream into soft peaks and fold in. Transfer to ice cream maker and process according to manufacturer's instructions.

Available at specialty food shops

ICED PLUM PUDDING

Serves 8

"Iced puddings are indispensable on fashionable
supper-tables and at dinner-parties."

½ a vanilla bean	¼ cup raisins
½ cup milk	¼ cup currants
2 cups heavy cream	2 tablespoons candied lemon peel
½ cup sugar	
½ cup almond paste	½ cup strawberry or raspberry preserves
2 tablespoons almond liqueur, curacao or brandy	
	1 cup chopped glace fruit
½ teaspoon nutmeg	
4 egg yolks	Whole glace fruits for garnish

Split vanilla bean, cut into 1-inch pieces, then scald in milk.
Strain and discard bean. Return milk to pan. Add cream (1 cup),
sugar, almond paste, liqueur and nutmeg and simmer 5 minutes.
Beat egg yolks until thick and add to pan. Now simmer over low
heat 2 minutes, stirring constantly. Dredge raisins, currants and
lemon peel in flour and stir into mixture. Cool. Stir in the
preserves and chopped fruit. Whip remaining cream until stiff
and fold into mixture. Spoon pudding into 1-quart rounded
bowl. Smooth top. Freeze 4 hours, then unmold on a platter.
Decorate with whole glace fruits before serving.

ORANGEADE ICE

Serves 4

1½ cups orange juice
½ cup powdered sugar

Peel from 3 oranges,
chopped

Combine juice and sugar with ½ cup water. Place peel in a bowl, pour in the liquid, cover, and let stand 1 hour. Refrigerate until well chilled. Strain, then transfer to ice cream maker and process as manufacturer directs.

CANDY

MOLASSES CANDY
Yields about 2 pounds

2 cups molasses	Grated rind and juice of 1 lemon
1 cup brown sugar	1 cup unsalted, dry-roasted peanuts

Combine molasses and sugar in large pot and bring to boil over moderate heat. Cook 2½ hours, stirring frequently and removing foam from surface. Add lemon rind, juice and peanuts and boil a further 30 minutes. Pour into buttered square pan and let stand to cool and set.

CHEESE

A WELSH RABBIT

¾ cup grated Cheddar cheese	Cayenne pepper
1 tablespoon butter	¼ cup red wine
1 teaspoon prepared mustard	8 slices toast, crust removed

Combine cheese, butter, mustard, cayenne and wine in a fireproof skillet and cook, while stirring, over low heat. Continue until mixture is creamy smooth. Quickly butter half the toast slices and arrange in a square on a shallow dish. Butter and set aside remaining toast. Put skillet into oven, under hot broiler, until cheese is lightly browned. Remove from oven and slide cheese from skillet onto the dish of toast. Serve at once, accompanied by the additional toast.

A CORDIAL

NOYAU

1 pint vodka
1 cup sugar
¼ cup honey
2 tablespoons almond extract

Grated rind of 1 lemon
4 tablespoons rosewater*
Red food coloring

Combine vodka, sugar, honey, almond extract and lemon rind in preserving jar with tight lid. Shake several seconds each day for a month. Let stand 60 days. Strain, then add rosewater and several drops of food coloring — and stir vigorously. Bottle and store. Serve as a cordial.

*Available at specialty food stores.

A COLD REMEDY

STEWED QUAKER

A cold remedy

1 cup molasses	½ teaspoon ginger
4 tablespoons butter	Juice of 1 lemon

Blend molasses, butter and ginger in a saucepan and cook 30 minutes over low heat. Stir frequently. Remove from heat, stir in lemon juice, cover, and let stand 5 minutes. Take it warm for best effect in treating a cold.

DECORATIONS & GLAZE FOR PIES

Miss Leslie was very fond of decorated and glazed meat pies. The attractive adornments are made from leftover pastry trimmings.

Small diamond shapes make rose leaves. Decorate by drawing a line down the center, with a knife point, and add some angular strokes as leaf veins. Moisten the back of each piece, curl it slightly and press it onto the pie crust. Larger shapes will do for oak leaves, but these must have edges in a scallop shape.

To make roses, cut ½-inch deep by 4-inch long strips and roll them into a spiral. Now pinch out petal shapes from the sides of the circle. Moisten one side of each form and press it onto the crust — at intervals between leaf shapes.

Acorns are made from little balls of dough, elongated and pointed by using your fingers. The top end is then moistened to receive a thin wrap-around strip to form the cup. Decorate the cup by pricking and scoring with a fork.

Scrolls and lattice effects are traditionally popular. These are made with narrow strips laid across the pie in a geometric pattern. The strips can be twisted or rolled to suit your fancy.

For the glaze, take one egg-white and blend it with a teaspoon of powdered sugar, while whisking briskly. Brush this over the crust and ornaments before baking.

BIBLIOGRAPHY

Seventy-Five Receipts for Pastry, Cakes and Sweetmeats by a Lady of Philadelphia. (Miss Eliza Leslie) New York, 1828

Domestic French Cookery, chiefly translated from Sulpice Barue, by Miss (Eliza) Leslie. Philadelphia, 1832

Directions for Cookery by Miss (Eliza) Leslie. Philadelphia, 1837

The Indian Meal Book by Miss (Eliza) Leslie. Philadelphia, 1847

The Lady's Receipt Book by Miss (Eliza) Leslie. Philadelphia, 1847

Miss Leslie's Lady's New Receipt Book. Philadelphia, 1850

More Receipts by Miss (Eliza) Leslie. Philadelphia, 1852

New Receipts for Cooking by Miss (Eliza) Leslie. Philadelphia, 1854

Miss Leslie's New Cookery Book. Philadelphia, 1857

INDEX

INDEX